w
michigan writers cooperative press
2023 poetry contest

UPSTAIRS, LISTENING
Melinda LePere

*To Marti —
Enjoy your
birthday.
Mindy LePere*

Melinda LePere

Michigan
WRITERS

Michigan Writers Cooperative Press
P. O. Box 2355
Traverse City, Michigan 49685

ISBN-13: 978-1-950744-12-1

Book cover by Amy Hansen
Book interior by Daniel Stewart

Contents

To Phil, always.

Upstairs, Listening
poems

What then may I do
but to cleave to what cleaves me.

Li-Young Lee

Amputations

The ring finger of grandfather's right hand, clean cut
just above the knuckle, was the one I held. The nub,
smooth as the velvet on a spring stag's horn,
if stroked, vibrated a plaintive itch—like fur
rubbed the wrong way—if thumped,
throbbed like a new bobbed tail.

I know the feeling. On our hitch-hiking honeymoon
midway across the Sahara, the truck,
gripped by a drift of sand, upended.
I catapulted through the windshield—
finger severed, grandmother's golden ring lost—
under that vast and faultless sky.

For my father it was different. He kept his thumb by allowing
the machine's severing blade to complete its circuit,
clutched the looseness of it fastened by a slip of skin,
tight within his fist. Reattached, it was as if he had cheated
the sacrifice—our cleavings like unaware animals
offered up to some primal force as the cost of passage.

I can scan a hand from across a room.
At the Harley Museum, I sidle up to the three-fingered
construction worker, exchange stories like trading cards.
You might think
it's the cataclysm that connects us
but it's the transition

to marvel in the missing that attracts me.
The way a glove reports a vacancy. Three fingers
adjust to tap the keys. The singing presence
of a molecular echo—a trick
of the nervous system—keeping me attached
to an absence.

Whistling for the Dark

Sometimes, window down,
fingers drumming the metal wing,
my father's whistle
warbled a mockingbird's trill, meshed
with the radio and gusting wind. But

he could lash it like a whip—
his shaft of tongue curved tight-tipped
in his cave of teeth—
the whistle's sharp summons
and we, gypsy children

under shadow elms, would run
the long block home. Then came
the night. Straggled hair
matted on sheets, soap
scrubbed cheeks, press
of kiss, moths

pulsing the screen,
the clasp and seal
of closing fridge, a click and lock,
the glider's rasp, my father in sway
under the awning, his lips

pillowed O, the whistle
uncoiling a Johnny Mercer tune—
its heat nuzzling
mother's neck, claiming
something beneath
our ordinary skin.

Snow Day

Awakening beneath the baffled roof
feels like Christmas when I still believed.
Straining for clues of arrival or exit,
drifting on nerves—more open with each
exhale to a time just south of night's center.

Outside, snow shrouds the constant crescendo.
No waves of traffic flow by—no pan-slam
of empty trailers, the lumbering whine
of trucks—no sounds remain in the displaced air.
On a snow day
everything is muffled—a lovely absent sound.
I can hear the air, the slow calcification
of walls and rafters. Downstairs,
someone monitors closings. Have I always been
upstairs, listening?
                        A vacuum rumbles,
a mother sings. Do you remember
opening the door, the world white and stopped,
a lopsided snow family, their thin twig arms,
the cold cut on skin as snow wedged,
hardened in any crease, the clunk as lumps
fell, the pin-prick warmth of my mother's
fingers, her breath? Inside,

                        there is a low hum—
something electrical, a soft fuzz
of slow evaporation, the pinging sound
of beads from a fountain. Water drips
off a ledge. Hands scratch at a clock.
If I burrow my hearing ear into the pillow,
I attend the echo of my inner well.
Under hard ground, my dead turn in their sleep.

The Horses in My Head

When the surgeon tunneled through my left ear
to the nest of the sleeping tumor,
symmetrical pairings, bundled and sheathed
after the drum, were severed. Cut
the reins on one side and see what happens.

The open ear, skittish as a colt, noses the air—
a pointer tracking elusive scents of sound.

As for the abandoned one, even as the steady scalpel
made its descent, I had removed her halter.
I thought to mourn her silence, keep her
in a pasture of white smoke memory,
but instead, she roams at random, a revenant
loose within my head. The peripheral clatter
of cutlery, the patter of light-laced water
triggers her panic into howling static.

Even at rest she resonates a rustling phantom hum:
a sift of wind in golden poplars, leaves
thrumming at the end of their stems.
When the sound is immense,
I surrender as a rock, accept a pounding
that finally ebbs. But, if I'm in luck,
I lie on the floor of her blue forest,
shadows glimmering invented sounds above us.
Her muzzle stirring silver grass.
Her ghost eye vast and vacant.

Mono No Aware

1.
A Japanese phrase surfaces

in my clippings—cryptic messages from my mother—if only
I could read them. It first fluttered up
                                        in National Geographic as

the persistence of snow cranes in the slim margin of winter—
            necks entwined,   beaks open.

2.
M. Bissonet, a Frenchman of a certain weight, a reclaimer
of invented instruments, flaunts

                my father's scrupulous nose.

Snake-shaped woodwinds in autumn hues. A three-necked
Harpophonium disgorging three pigeons. As a child,
            he tapped symphonies on his teeth.

My father was a whistler, but
                        I never dream in sound.

3.
Mono no aware captions the still of a blurred ghost—
        a shadow
                wearing a kimono
                        attending a picnic. Her hand

blends into the hand
            of her husband's new wife. They reach
                                    for a pear.

4.
A mad recluse maps the confluence of the mundane
and the cataclysmic, arcs and ovals

                curve and coil

                        on every wall—meanwhile, in Paris,

        Louise Bourgeois draws herself to sleep—

sweeping ellipses,
                        spiraling vortexes,
                                        forests of circles

mound and collapse—her pencil pulled
                        by the gravity of dreams.

5.
Red ribbons,
        attached to the eyes of a scorched puppet maiden,
                                        unspool.

Across the stage,
                the Hiroshima bomber
                        begs for their binding.

Clowns from Bali mediate between the dead who shout—

Don't watch me! I'm not here!
                        and the mourners
                                who can't turn away.

6.

                the pivot in a Tonka—
                mono no aware—
                a tenderness touching

MELINDA LEPERE

In Cuba, I Wait For My Mother

As always, I am diverted.
Up a spiral staircase
at the Pink Poodle Lounge,
notes perch—yellow parakeets
on wrought iron railings.
My husband wears
a white tuxedo. At a glass table,
a French waitress
in a black tulip skirt
serves my daughters. One
is blond; the other, a soft gray mouse,
laps from a white saucer bordered
by blue forget-me-nots. In the golden light,
a greedy tenderness.

A field is mowed into rays.
At the end of a dusty road
I arrive at my mother's beach.
Waves pound. I lead her,
bloated and undiagnosed, into the sea.
Sand shifts. Unbalanced,
she clings to me. We stumble
to our cabana, bleached and frayed.

She extends an open hand,
but her eyes focus on something distant.
I am left, listening for her echo—
a thrown stone, forever falling,
after all the ripples
have reached the shore.

What Breath

Almost spring   when air

    still fogs   and ready trees

unkink

   and blush

       hues so lush

          yet slant

a hard consideration   could turn right back

   to winter

    —ghosts' breath—

the lean-in   to light   her angled cigarette

  smoke

     pools on my mother's lips

before   the deep inhale   slow release

  smoke   another language

above   starlings   in murmuration

    stir the air

MELINDA LEPERE

Ordinary Myth

Hephaestus, the one who can figure things out,
drives a wood-paneled station wagon. He bears
the smoky musk of perpetual coal. Forget Aphrodite—
he rides with Hestia, keeper of the hearth.
She concentrates on the road, hits
panic brakes on the dash, wills
a destination. Hephaestus's eyes
never leave the rearview mirror
nailing unbuckled children to the hot vinyl seat.

After the monotony of I-94,
in the labyrinth of a tidy trailer park
far from Olympus, Hestia
swats mosquitoes, cooks
in a cramped cabana.

On Saturdays, Homer calls square dances in the barn,
tilts his head to stomping twirls his almost singing voice
guides home. Across the summer ice of Lake Huron,
lies Sarnia. Depend upon Old Uncle Odysseus,
retelling tales of sweet, smuggled whiskey, to once again
abandon land.

Hephaestus stokes a frail watch-fire.
The lame leg aches. On the eroding cliff,
marshmallow torches flame to ash.
In the all-dark, waves rise—
wild-maned remnants of Poseidon's herd.

Building the Horse

Regret is the broken leg from my little knickknack horse,
lost so long ago. The dead are gone—ghost inventions
that focus and fade. There were slipcovers my mother sewed
to hide the couch. In the morning there was lumpy
Cream of Wheat, the Bible, and retold Perry Mason mysteries.
My father's teeth, milk and meat. His tracks in the snow—
Lucky smoke threading from behind the garage.
I can give you endings: something with his heart, her cancer.
They come back to me in residual fog, a shift of dust
stirred by a vacuum, stale, unsettled—
the weight of ash.

        In the time it takes to mourn I have been productive.
        Tattered elegies drafted. Tinder gathered.

I thought there would be time to know them but,
like them, I was busy—burying the past. That I am not
my mother was once what mattered most to me.
It's not about remembering since theirs are stories
I never heard. I don't want help
like sentimental photos, my siblings' accuracy.
I have tried dreaming them. Extrapolate and polish
some small gleanings—stones and toothy shells
like the ones once gathered at the beach,
vague summers at the lake—
broken boats wash up on the shore.

        Charred driftwood, canting in lamenting waves,
        salvaged. I shape the planks.

There were so many hidden places
my father built to organize and contain.
Open this one to find a meter ticking,
arrays of player piano rolls. Or this low cabinet,
close to the floor, crawl in and find lost books.
The Dog Who Belonged to Himself among the Little Goldens,
beneath them a book on the cosmos—unfold the page

MELINDA LEPERE

of chaos and creation. I want to be clear
but I'm getting confused. Someone is weeping.
Listen. Hear my father's whistle, my mother's murmur.
On the shifting sand I bend and gather,
cobble the legs until I drag my almost horse
up to my Trojan Wall. The dead open wide the gates.

       I will never get them back.
       I raise the ax to loot and sack.

It is Sunday

he looks up,
pink cheeked, fresh shaven. Already
there are clear beads of perspiration
on his forehead. Dad had the cleanest sweat.
It is before the family foray to church
where he wears a Sears suit and polished shoes.
His Old Spice smells like a night-time man
but he is at the breakfast stove in a white t-shirt
holding a black iron skillet, browning flour
in Crisco and bacon grease, his precise ratio.

We are complicit cooks. I catch him—
his eyebrow raised, a wink of hazel eye.
I am measuring
the Bisquick. He never breaks
concentration—a steady scrape
to a metronome heartbeat
from another kitchen
making milk gravy, poor man's food

once packed in pails his brothers carried
down to the mines, now, our Sunday treat.
Sun glimmers his freckles, laces shadows
through the short black hairs on his arm.
My father's temper, forever gnawing on perfection,
crouches in a corner, asleep, I hope.
A sharp sizzle as milk hits the pan.
Biscuits just right, golden brown
and tapping done. They pull apart,
soft and vulnerable, open to margarine
pooling up
through thick white gravy
spiked with pepper.

MELINDA LEPERE

Secrets

In the morning it is church,
stiff and starched, a place of high light,
chartreuse and rust, a dormant scent,

lavender, lily of the valley—locked
in a drawer. Open a hymnal to thin sheets.
Bend the binding to tunnel something

breathing beneath the organ.
A pot roast matured during the service,
then we mashed them—potatoes.

Ate the carrots—seared and tender.
Sunday supper in the dining room.
On the high shelf of the little hutch,

out of reach in a grandmother teacup,
little gumballs rattled—a penny each
after groceries. I only wanted

to crack the shell of dark red cinnamon
            so close to sin.   Sin
smells like Clorox or the coughing dust

the vacuum thrusts and leaves
hovering on the carpet—rises to ghost
in slanted sunlight. Some sin

rinses away—an astringent squeak.
Mother cups my head under the faucet
and pours the cider vinegar, my body

limp on maroon tile, dark
as dry blood. Accidents and leakages,
the smell of feral metal—

caustic as urine on unwashed underwear.
Coiled in bed I am clean, attend shadows,
glimpse the elf's silhouette, dolls

in plastic shrouds. A mirror my mother made,
encrusted with shells and plastic jewels,
funnels the moon.

In Matters of Faith

                              my mother kept
an open heart. Below the Methodist Jesus
praying in Gethsemane
hung the muscle of a Bleeding Heart—
gift from a Catholic neighbor—
dangling a Mary medallion, saints and healing charms.

Every morning it was a verse from her mother's Bible,
a meditation from the Daily Word—the weekly order
held in hymns stringing us to heaven. Once,

                              I was a soprano,
clear as a bell, now, off key, I rasp along
once a year. Yet, the organ in fortissimo—
ponderous thunder grounded in the pedalboard
vibrates something buried. Easter Sundays,

                              glissandos swirling above us,
matching in dresses I had begged her to make,
her arm about me, I would mold into my mother.
Rimmed in rippled light we exclaimed
Halleluiah, Amen—our breath a song—
the open throats of fledglings in the nest,
the comfort of the fold.

Self Portrait, Fox Under Glass

After a painting by Viviana Hinjosa

One of my eyes, a girl's eye,
long lashed above a rouged cheek—
enigmatic in my forever fox face—
watches from a bell jar. I wear
a russet dress barred in muted stripes,
the collar white cotton eyelet,
a soft trim my mother might have sewn.
Look at my legs—
stockinged like a jumpy doll, pink and indigo,
the straps and buckles of my Mary Janes.
My props, twigs fixed in a dirtish foundation, bent
by the curve of the glass. On the knobbed cover
a swatch of light repels the outer world.

Within, a moon hovers above me. Is this about
confinement? Is every family
a kind of prison? A small house cobbles up at my feet
one of the toadstools that pop up in this place.
Incandescent lures, will-o-the-wisps,
haunt the woods—a tangle of trails
shifting like synapses. There is no limit
to this bark and bone forest.

In my hand, yes, my human hand (only my head
is feral) I hold a corked flask—decanted memories
glow like captured fireflies, flicker, while I
stand the night. I was not raised by wolves
but longed to be one. Consider my other eye,
a concave nest of infinite stars.

MELINDA LEPERE

Proximity with a Travel Magazine in Quarantine

In this distancing time, words on the page
become precious. I am held by narratives,
attach to random burs of clinging facts—

when I read it, I hear it—
a phantom singing in the shift of sand,
the essay's mirage—a distant city everyone sees

wavering next to them on the parched remnants
of the Silk Road. I find myself longing
for unpronounceable land-locked cities,

blue towers tiled to challenge the sky, longing
for their chaotic pasts. The overlay of names
that once covered the gateway—a record

of ancient exiles—whitewashed. Why
does this erasure give me such grief?
Curses, contagions, plagues—ours,

of course—the dead forgotten. Mass graves
lost in the margins of war and conquest.
Language dies as well, some common word

unpurposed, misplaced. I have to take notes.
A temblor sheared a mountain unveiling
ancient caves—their walls covered

in undulating frescoes, and someone—
a trader, a pilgrim—so entranced by their beauty,
entered into them. For centuries, the Buddha

was carved without features, here, palm raised,
his eyes are full of sand, his face
a cloud without the vehemence of rain. Of 3000

broken clay guardians, somehow re-pieced,
all are found to be unique—*only from a distance
were they an army, in proximity, each*

a separate man. And then there is silk.
Consider, a Roman battalion in disarray,
defeated by their first sighting of something radiant

unfurling in the sky—its billow shaping,
shifting. An old woman instructs, *Each silkworm
is concerned only with its own journey.*

I believe they are blind, these worms.
Somewhere it said—passage on this road
could change you so profoundly

you might never again
be welcomed home.

MELINDA LEPERE

(Parkinson's)

There is a language that lingers in our hands—
I have held his for over fifty years. In tandem,
we stroll Paris in search of rumored puppets
he would find for me. Up an almost ally,
at the window of a closed boulangerie,
a few have gathered. A tiny world
presents before us:

white kerchiefs billow and dive,
cloud into storm. We will see
a small tragedy. The puppeteer's hands
become a queen with a dangle of hair,
a warrior with a swatch of plaid.
The little characters
absurd. We grin and nudge each other.

But begin to feel it—the limits of this world—
the powers above. Ghosts wait and watch.
A crow, transformed from black handled
secateurs, undulates in oracular flight,
the slow snipping beak, the pivot
of its eye. The thunder of cheap
kitchen knives clatter and clang.
Their smallness—the cloth-soft limit

of each fated motion.
And now his hand will squeeze mine
because he knows me,
the staggered tremors
will renew their agitation
and we will strain to contain
the flailing animal fighting for release.

Little Mummies Tucked Under Blankets in the Back—

we were packaged for the triple feature at the drive-in.
My parents thought the children would sleep through
but sometime in the *Village of the Damned*, I woke up.
All the boys and girls, each so blond and neat, all of them
paying attention, just like me, until their eyes
began to glow. And there, in the hearse-like rear
of the paneled station wagon, I peeked over and so
was pierced. I had shifted a rock that could never be
reset. Something

tunneled in. Once on vacation, we floated across an empty
Utah highway in a great sea-foam Mercury sedan,
back window descending. It was movie-telling time,
The Birds. My mother's hand, with the wing-like lift
of a conductor's baton, cued the inexplicable flock,
punctuated their bloody beaks, kept us
pressed to our seats. In twilight, the car rushed ahead
as a furred cloud crashed upon us. An exhalation of bats,
bats we outraced and later found impaled in the grill.

One New Year's Eve, while adults partied above us,
it was *Invasion of the Body Snatchers* and I couldn't tell
who had been taken. You couldn't fall asleep or
you would lose yourself. Something alien ticked away,
gnawing inside. An ordinary monster,
that's what incubated. Like that *Bad Seed* girl tap-tapping
her patent leather shoes up the cellar steps,
or the eerie doll in the *Twilight Zone*, scuttling
to a shadow place, an oven door slapping open,
clapping shut.

Inside the Cathedral

                              someone is practicing.
The organ repeats a run, pounding
walls of stone. Notes crash
flash to the rafters. A riptide
rumbles below. Where do they find rest,
those wayward notes?

Look at the constellations—connected dots of mammoth stars
and all the dark awash between, like shadows framed
by a nighttime door. Once, my brother
colored a family portrait—manila paper coated
solid black. He explained we were all there
in his room behind a black curtain.

Hear the father's chuckle, the murmur
of children, the shuffle of cards,
the slap and scratch
as they gather tricks
across a midnight table.

On an Anniversary

More than 40. Wait, let me check:
he says, *You ask every year.*
It is 44 and, *Why don't you remember?*
and I say, *because you do.*
We are searching for something

at the bottom of the junk drawer.
Among the unhinged sticky notes
is an old list of things to do, undated,
still timely. Here is a lapel pin from
his union days, long days, longer nights
negotiated in tandem. There is an
expired horoscope that still sums us up:
Taurus and Gemini. He, steadfast
and bullish on me while I
prevaricate and baffle both of us.
Bits and pieces of games we played,
singlets from scrabble, words we
had the sense not to say, unmatched
dice—the kind we never gambled with.
Our luck stocked up for our children.

Beneath loose pinochle cards, a copy
of my mother's obituary and I can
smell the Florida night of her death,
the sky cloudless. Looking up, I saw
the climax of a shooting star. *Look!*
I cried. *Its mom meeting dad.* My hand
in his, he hesitated, then murmured, *I think*
it was an arcing transformer. I pick

a square case that pivots open: a magnifier
I took to be a compass. At least I will be able
to read those fine print maps always creased
on something important. He checks a palm-sized
compact tin. It is a retractable measuring tape
from my father's pocket. Always
at the ready. We have forgotten
what we were looking for.

MELINDA LEPERE

Watching the Garden

My husband introduces me
to each new blossom,
Look who's here! and I step
to the driveway edge. Pant legs
wet with dew, untucked shirt
damp, softened by dirt,
he leans on his shovel.
Deadheads and invasives
mounded near the coral bells, he awaits
my benediction. The nasturtiums

are my favorite but
when the honeysuckle and lilac bloom
I am in my mother's yard—
her back bent, crouched
over the weeding—the roses
that resisted her. She would
cut a bouquet and arrange
a small still life that never stayed still
if plush peonies were in the bowl. Petals
flounced by ants so small—their purpose

so particular. How they clung—
their tiny trace awakening
the skin—body flush
of pin-prick memory.   Her hand
cupping their softness. Inhaling
lush scent.   My husband
has peonies too. They tend
to bend under their weight,
bowed to earth
exhausted by their beauty.

In Florida, the Immersive van Gogh

streams around me. Symphonic music punctuates—
there will be no doubt when the sorrows begin—
and there are my mother's irises pixilating into sunflowers and I
sense her presence beside me as I resist
the directives of the orchestra.

It was very large
the scarf I gave my mother. Vincent's
indigo irises, green diagonal stalks
rippling on a citron field—dense yellow
on thick silk. She could carry it off—
a shoulder drape secured
with a practical knot. Back then, we walked
curved paths under moss-draped trees,
water glinting on the bay beyond the breakwater,
and when her steps faltered
we returned to her room. From the window,
she imagined a shadow man
propped against a palm tree. His threat
impersonal but constant.

I am alone at the exhibit. Yellow, always hers,
the color I would never have chosen, chooses me.
Within the yellow strokes I now like best,
there is never hesitation—only the engulfing
pleasure of the paint, thick and lavish and yet,
within are hairlines of red and green—
yellow containing their terrible passions.
In the last paintings, brick-like strokes
wall the canvas, chaotic clouds
swirl, crows tangle like worms.

A cancer grew within her.
The path became dizzy and decomposed.
His bedroom resonates with hers—a suffusion of light,
a contentment in solitude, the alignment
of small pleasures. Always, there were flowers
stationed in a vase.

MELINDA LEPERE

Child's Portrait of Dog

On four stiff legs, the lone dog almost smiles.
The open handle of his unheld leash
floats in echo of a happy hollow sun. All the dogs
who ever rested in this room carried the same name,
were nestled in place before
Good night, turn out the light, before the child arm
hooked the mother's neck.

My granddaughter lifts her hand, small palm open
to this moment's billion fallen cells. Which mother
strokes the blossom skin? Who breathes
in resonance? Fingers spread,
we turn our wrists in purl and knit,
lacing air.

Someone Might Call and Call

                    but you have forgotten—

suppertime twilight
sliced by a father's shrill whistle.

A child is beguiled
by a soft nest of darkness—
a pile of parent coats
mounded on a mother's bed. And you,
burrowing into synthetic folds, rough wool,
New Year party fur, inhaling
snow cloud, stagnant smoke,
Midnight in Paris.

Listen, someone is rhyming
a ball against the house,
increasing the claps,
avoiding the cracks.
The hands that linked
in dinner prayer
all release.

Behind the cherry tree's
thin trunk crouches a child,
holding the string to a trap,
a clothespin propping a box.
But those side-eyed memory birds
will not be lured. They fly away
to another continent of the brain.
Spits of ink imagined into wing—
vapor birds
above the amber trees.
Remember me.

MELINDA LEPERE

Notes

"The Horses in my Head": Acoustic Neuroma is a non-cancerous tumor that affects the nerves leading from the inner ear to the brain.

"Mono No Aware": A Japanese phrase that means "the fragile sadness of things."

Acknowledgements

The Collagist   "Inside the Cathedral"

The MacGuffin   "Building the Horse"
                          "The Horses in My Head"
                          "Whistling for the Dark"

Mantis   "In Cuba"

Metro Times   "Ordinary Myth

Valparaiso Poetry Review "Amputations"

Zoetic Press   "A Sense of Secrets"

About the Judge

Michigan Writers Cooperative Press would like to express our thanks to JENNIFER SPERRY STEINORTH. Jennifer's books include *A Wake with Nine Shades* (2019) and *Her Read, A Graphic Poem* (2021), recipient of *Foreword Review*'s bronze prize in poetry and Texas Institute of Letters' Fred Whitehead Award for Design. She lectures at the University of Michigan and is a 2023-2024 Beinecke Fellow at Yale, conducting research for a biography of C.D. Wright. Scholarly work on Wright is forthcoming from the University of Michigan Press and elsewhere and her poetry appears or is forthcoming from *The Cincinnati Review, Denver Quarterly Review, Kenyon Review, Missouri Review, Pleiades, Plume, RHINO* and *TriQuarterly*. An alum of Interlochen Arts Academy, her interdisciplinary approach to language is drawn from years as a classical dancer and a decade in architectural design and construction. She has served on the Michigan Writers Board of Directors and divides her time between Ann Arbor and Traverse City, Michigan.

About the Author

Melinda (Mindy) has been an assembler in a Russian watch factory, a paralegal, a telephone installer, and a teacher. She is the mother of two daughters and a world traveler who once hitchhiked across the Sahara during her extended honeymoon. As a Detroit elementary school teacher, she partnered with InsideOut and facilitated an annual Family Poetry Night.

Mindy holds an MFA from Vermont College and is a member of Springfed Arts and Detroit Women Writers. She has been published in numerous journals. Mindy's affinity for the surreal manifests in a fascination with puppets, memory, fairy tales and the ordinary strangeness of life.

She lives with her husband, a fellow Michigan State University alum, in Detroit.

About Michigan Writers Cooperative Press

This book was published in the spring of 2023 in a signed edition of 100 copies.

This chapbook is part of the Cooperative Series of the Michigan Writers Small Press Project, which was launched in 2005 to give members of Michigan Writers, Inc. a new avenue to publication. All of the chapbooks in this series are an author's first book in that genre. The Coop Press shoulders the publishing costs for the first edition, and writers share the marketing and promotional responsibilities in return for the prestige of being published by a press that prints only carefully selected manuscripts.

Chapbook length manuscripts of poetry, short stories, and essays are solicited each year from members and adjudicated by a panel of experienced writers and a judge who is a specialist in a particular genre. For more information, please visit www.michwriters.org.

MICHIGAN WRITERS is an open-membership organization dedicated to providing opportunities for networking, professional growth, and publication for writers of all ages and skill levels in Northwest Michigan and beyond.

MANAGING EDITOR: Gail Wallace Bozzano

BOOK DESIGN: Amy Hansen, Daniel Stewart

Other Titles Available
from Michigan Writers Cooperative Press

The Grace of the Eye by Michael Callaghan
Trouble With Faces by Trinna Frever
Box of Echoes by Todd Mercer
Beyond the Reach of Imagination by Duncan Spratt Moran
The Grass Impossibly by Holly Wren Spaulding
The Chocolatier Speaks of his Wife by Catherine Turnbull
Dangerous Exuberance by Leigh Fairey
Point of Sand by Jaimien Delp
Hard Winter, First Thaw by Jenny Robertson
Friday Nights the Whole Town Goes to the Basketball Game
        by Teresa J. Scollon
Seasons for Growing by Sarah Baughman
Forking the Swift by Jennifer Sperry Steinorth
The Rest of Us by John Mauk
Kisses for Laura by Joan Schmeichel
Eat the Apple by Denise Baker
First Risings by Michael Hughes
Fathers and Sons by Bruce L. Makie
Exit Wounds by Jim Crockett
The Solid Living World by Ellen Stone
Bitter Dagaa by Robb Astor
Crime Story by Kris Kuntz
Michaela by Gabriella Burman
Supposing She Dreamed This by Gail Wallace Bozzano
Line and Hook by Kevin Griffin
And Sarah His Wife by Christina Diane Campbell
Proud Flesh by Nancy Parshall
Angel Rides a Bike by Margaret Fedder
Ink by Kathleen Pfeiffer
What Will You Teach Her? by Megan Klco Kellner
Bluetongue and Other Michigan Stories by Ryan Shek
The Mountain Ash by Kathleen Rabbers
This Blue Earth by Sharon Bippus
Upstairs, Listening by Melida LePere
Twinkies by Kathleen Quigley
The Sound a Car Door Makes by Natalie Tomlin

**Michigan
WRITERS**

CPSIA information can be obtained
at www.ICGtesting.com
Printed in the USA
JSHW020805230523
42085JS00001B/17

9 781950 744121